Forbidden Fruit

Tales of Love, Lust, & Loss

Crystle Castle

Forbidden Fruit

ISBN: 9798218087975

Published by Electric Girl Enterprises, LLC

www.electricgirlpoetry.com

IG: @electricgirpoetry

Cover Art by Ken Koberlein
IG: @ken_koeber

Edited by Vanessa Dremè

To M.,

You helped me learn that love is not possession;
love is freedom.
Thank you for the lessons, the pleasure, and the pain.
Thank you for inspiring my first book, and above all else,
for reminding me again and again of my worth.

With Love,
-C.

ACKNOWLEDGMENTS

A sincere thank you to all my friends and family who have supported me on my writing journey! A very special thanks to Taylor, Mitchy, Candis, & Lou, who answered my distress calls and shined a light on me during my darkest days. Thank you for believing in me and encouraging me to press on when I felt like giving up.

Thank you to my dear friends, Bob and Linda Brammer, for their unwavering support and encouragement. A special thanks to Farmer Tom for being my biggest fan and always supporting my work.

To my grandparents, Judy and Wayne Jambois, thank you for your love, reassurance, and support.

Much appreciation to the graphic design artist who created this beautiful cover, Ken Koeberlein, and to the editor, Vanessa Dremè.

I am deeply humbled and grateful that so many people believe in me. Your kindness, generosity, and optimism have helped me to accomplish one of my lifelong goals.

With Gratitude,
Crystle

PREFACE

The muse for this book was a married man I call "M." who, for a time, I shared an intimate relationship with. It was a whirlwind romance; hot and heavy, and oh so horribly wrong, though it felt so incredibly right!

These pages are filled with all of my deepest, darkest poetry and prose; the fruits of my labor of blood, sweat, and tears. They allude to our sordid affair; the temptation, the passion, and the excruciating heartache of forbidden love.

This book is for those who couldn't resist the alluring taste of forbidden fruit. It is for those who have been kept a secret, who have fallen prey to unrequited love, or who have experienced the confusion, frustration, and heart-wrenching fate of being "the other woman."

Falling in love is like falling into the sea– exciting, terrifying, and deeply mysterious. One will be, at times, drowning and breathless, and at others, buoyant and mercifully full of life. I pray this book helps you fall into the ocean of love with yourself. May you ride the waves, catch your breath, and find hope and healing in these pages.

~Crystle Castle

Stories

Tell me
a story
of love and pain…

Make me feel alive
once again.

Spooked

There I was, minding my own business, just nibbling on some grass. Spring had just sprung, so I was hungrily hunting for those little green sprouts popping up here and there. The forest ground was still damp with thawing snow as I slowly made my way through the trees.

Suddenly, I heard a noise, so I perked my ears up and became very still, trying to discern what it could be. It was more than a rustle, but quieter than the wind blowing through the leaves. I heard the crunch of a twig breaking, the faint sound of snow being softly trampled, and then my nose wiggled as it caught the undeniable scent of a man on the breeze. All at once, I knew what it was. It was a hunter, coming through the forest to look for my kind.

I had seen them before and had been shot at a time or two. One almost killed me, but luck had been on my side. I was young and agile then, and I'd gotten away. I now knew that men were very dangerous, and they meant to kill and eat me if they could. So, I stood there, trying to blend in with the trees, standing perfectly still, not moving a muscle. Then I saw a movement out of the corner of my eye, and he came into view.

There was something about the look in his eyes… something captivating. As we made eye contact my heart dropped down into my stomach and I knew I was done for. He was too close for me to run away, and it was no use trying to hide— my cover was blown. So, we stood there, side by side, the two of us, staring into each other's eyes, and something deep within me seemed to say, *"Don't run."* His eyes said, *"Don't be afraid."*

I don't know what possessed me to just stand there like a dumb animal, because even though most men thought that's what I was, the truth is I was, in fact, a magical creature. This whole forest was magical, although most of the magic had dwindled away with the loggers cutting down the biggest and oldest trees, and the fairies and gnomes moving underground into hiding, and most of the witches having been burned at the stake long ago.

Nevertheless, I froze. My instincts took over and I simply couldn't help myself. As he slowly made his way toward me, he offered me his outstretched hand. In it was something that looked like food, and I realized I was hungry. The winter had been long and hard, and food had been scarce. If I'm being honest, I wasn't just hungry — *I was starving.*

This hunter wasn't like the others. They all held weapons, but this one was different. Instead of attacking me, he offered me something instead. And maybe that's why I did it. I let him walk right up to me, and I ate that food straight from his outstretched hand. It was good... *really* good. It tasted sweet, like the sweetest berries ripened in the summer sun. And as he fed me, he gently reached out and started to stroke and pet me as no one had ever done before.

That's how it began: a deer fell in love with a hunter, and you can probably guess what happened next. After I had my fill, and my belly was warm and full, he pulled me close, and I nestled into his chest to fall asleep. And that's when he stabbed me right in my beating heart.

But as fate would have it, he couldn't kill me, because he didn't know that I was magical. As he pulled his knife out and tried to lunge at me again, I managed to get up on my wobbly legs and run.

I ran and ran, slowly at first, but then faster as I felt the blood dripping down my chest. Soon enough it started to dry and the hole that was once there began to slowly close up.

After a time, I crossed a river and washed off the crusted blood from my aching heart, then found a cave to hide in. There I rested, hurting and healing for a long while. I didn't know if he was still chasing me, but by then I had managed to get far enough away that he hopefully couldn't track me anymore.

As I licked my wounds, I vowed that next time I'd be wiser. Next time, I wouldn't freeze. Next time, I'd be *spooked*.

The Physics of Heartstrings

I have a theory...
A heartstring theory.
Heartstrings are the strongest of strings.
Even when frayed and weak,
they will still cling to their lovers.

If you pluck them,
sometimes they sing sweet songs of love,
other times they sing melancholy tales of woe,
or soft lullabies that gently lull you to sleep.

The funny thing about heartstrings is
that their very nature is that of a string, rather than
a point of singularity.

This means that they often get tangled, caught, and
twisted, and sometimes they stick persistently
against your will.

They magically stretch through dimension, space,
and time.

Newtonian physics means nothing to heartstrings,
for they come from the ether,
causing spooky action at a distance.

Not physical, they,
though often their pull can cause physical pain.

Try as you might to cut these strings,
the more you'll begin to realize that resistance is
futile.

Heartstrings must fray and dissolve on their own.
No sword is sharp enough,
no distance is long enough;
no amount of radioactive substance
is radioactive enough
to kill the heart in Schrodinger's box,
or to sever the strings the heart makes.

Little Red String

What is this thing
That we're doing?
Looking, but not talking,
Wishing, but not acting?

What is this pattern
That keeps me
Yearning for you
Like a seed yearns for water;
Loving you,
When I should be running away?

What is this feeling
That keeps us coming back–
Keeps us spellbound
To an enchanted story
That we eagerly read
Again, and again,
Knowing full well the ending?

What is this little red string
'Round our little red hearts
That keeps us tied,
Tethered and bound,
With reckless abandon,
Mad and giddy,
Hopeless prisoners
To fickle love?

Ripe For the Picking

I'm ripe for the picking
plump, juicy, sweet,
and oh, so tender.

I'm ready to be tasted,
ready to be devoured.

What you see on the outside
is nothing
compared to
what's hidden–
all gooey sweetness
on the inside.

If you're worthy,
I'll envelop your senses.
I'll let you enter
this sacred garden
and savor
my forbidden fruit.

Beyond

Look beyond
what the eyes can see,

Feel with the wisdom
of your heart what is true.

Open the door of your soul
to me,

And I'll open mine
to you.

Sacred Geometry

Come
Drown your sorrows in me.
Let me catch your eye like a glint of sun.
Shift your attention
To the way all my curves align
In such sweet reunion–
A circle and a square,
Sacred geometry of shape and form.

Listen
To how my voice rings like a bell,
Beckoning you through the night,
Calling you through the mist,
Like an angel's song,
Or a siren's lure–
Either one will lead you
To me.

Watch
How I dance with such strange beauty;
A twist, a shimmy, a flick of the wrist,
To a slow, melodic rhythm
That only we can hear;
A gypsy's ring fingered call
That no hot blooded, two-legged
Could resist.

Feel
The peace that comes from stillness;
The slow creep of morning sun
Across a dark blue sky.
The gentle breeze of my breath
As it whispers and tickles your whiskers;
A tiny piece of heavenly reprieve
Reminding you that you're still alive.

Only One Thing

We caught each other's eyes,
And our hearts skipped beats like jump rope.
Liquid courage made me brave,
So, I took a leap of faith
And a shot of hope.

You said you weren't
Like every other man
Out to get "only one thing."
And you were smitten—
mesmerized—
By an angel like me.

I said my heart is too deep.
A one-night stand
Wouldn't satisfy my needs.
But both of our desires
Fed by devious thoughts
Began to grow,
Until the fire spread

Down deep and slow,
Consumed our flesh,
Revealed our bones.
Now you've become a ghost.
Shall we let this fire die?
A pity—an unturned lock with perfect key.
Now I'm left to burn alone,
A hot coal smoldering.

Gazing in your eyes,
Only one thing, I resist…
While longing to hear more sinful lies
Sweetly rolling off
Your devil lips.

Temptation

Oh, to be tempted!
To be lured by your
irresistible charms …
To be wrapped in your arms
and held in your embrace
is to sweetly perish
by the delicious kiss
of Death himself.

Expectations

I expect you to drop me,
For how could two hands ever hold
A heart and soul that seems to be
As soft and heavy as gold?

I expect you to leave me,
For what man could ever stay
With a woman so wickedly wild by night
And charmingly cunning by day?

I expect you to hurt me,
'Cause no one has gotten so close
Without laughing and smiling sweetly
While cutting me straight to the bone.

I expect you to walk away,
Not 'cause the grass is greener, babe,
But simply because
I wouldn't stand in your way.

I expect it all to be beautiful,
Delightful, magical, and sweet,
Right before it all crumbles
To rubble beneath my bare feet.

If the past predicts the future,
Then I know what I can expect,
So, for now I'll enjoy the ride
And see what happens next.

Wanting

I want to feel your soft kisses
on my forehead,
and your strong arms
holding me tight.

I want to fall asleep
with my head on your chest
while you're stroking my hair
in the moonlight.

I want you to tell me
all of your secrets; reveal all of your lies.
I want to know what makes you tick,
and all you try to hide.

I want to be the only one
you ever want and need.
I want to be the only girl
with whom you do the deed.

I want to give you
all of me–
all the things
no one sees.

I want you to give me
all of you–
let me see all
the bad stuff too.

I just want to hold your hand,
but I'll be damned—
all you want
is a one-night stand.

Look

"Look me in the eyes,"
he said,
as he tilted my chin
and lifted my head.

Little did we know,
that was
the beginning
of the inevitable end.

F w \ o B

You can come over,
But don't hug me too tight, or for too long.

Don't look at me with those eyes
That seem to stare right through me
All the way down into my soul.

Don't kiss me on the lips;
Don't even *dream* about tongue.

Don't get close enough
To smell my perfume,
Or put your hands in my hair.

Remain at a safe distance
And keep the conversation light.

Don't make funny little innuendoes,
Or give me sideways glances
With sexy smirks and flirtatious grins.

Definitely don't do that thing that you do
Where you just look so goddamn cute I can't
stand it.

In fact,
On second thought,
Who am I kidding?
Don't come over.

Intuition

"Run away,"
She said to herself.
"Put your sneakers on,
Lace those bitches up tight,
And run like a bear is chasing you."

Starry Sky

I want to get close,
But I know you'll leave
Just like all the others.
Just like my daddy left me.
Took his love away,
Made me a cliché…
Just like every other man
That I've loved–
I've given my all,
My everything,
And it was taken.
Greedily,
Hungrily,
Every last drop
Devoured
'Til there was nothing left of me
But a pile of broken glass–
Shards so sharp
They could pierce
A thousand and one holes
In an empty black sky.
So too, will you leave me.
You'll walk away
Feeling satisfied,
Smug and content,
With a belly full and warm.
And here, I'll remain
Shining like a dimly lit star
Until I burn out.

Bluebeard's Door

Don't open that door–
If you do, you're only going to see
A lot of macabre, twisted, and broken things.

Don't go in there–
You're not going to find
What you were looking for anyway.

Don't let
Your morbid curiosity
Override your common sense.

Don't let
Your desire for fun
Overcome your better judgment.

Don't dip
Your toes into the sea
Unless you plan on diving in.

Don't keep
Your head in the clouds
Reliving a fantasy.

Don't deny
You're clearly living
In a prison of your own design.

Don't take
That golden key
If you can't turn the lock.

Don't pretend
That playing with fire
Is innocent.

Don't get attached–
Don't think that this time
Will be any different.

Don't be deceived
By my smile,
Or my womanly wiles.

Don't open up
If you don't want me seeing
Right through your disguise.

Wishes

If wishes were horses,
Then beggars would ride.
If lovers were daydreams,
You'd be by my side.

Pandora's Box

Does he know what he's doing?
Or who he's messing with?
Opening Pandora's box
And waiting to see what happens?

Does he know what he's getting himself into?
Digging a hole deeper and deeper,
Thinking maybe one day
He'll find the bottom...

Does he know that he's playing
A dangerous game;
Lighting matches and watching them burn
All the way down to his fingertips?

Does he know
That Risk is a hungry lover
Who will compel him with her innocent kiss
And consume him with her deviant darkness?

Does he know that he's about to plunge
Headlong into a world of pain
Gilded with pleasure
And wrapped in a pretty little bow?

God, I hope not.

Stay

You have every reason
to walk away.
But baby,
I still want you to stay.

Spellbound

I'm Magick–
Are you spellbound yet?
I'm a little sprinkle of stardust
Bound in a body
And floating in space.
I'll say abracadabra
And make you love me.

I'm Magick–
I'll dance naked under moonlight
And seduce you by flames of fire.
I'll make a fancy potion
With eye of newt and hair of boar.
Don't bother running—
You can't escape the spell I've cast.

I'm Magick–
I'll wrap my snakes around you like chains,
And hold you close in my embrace;
Intoxicate you with the scent of my passion,
And paralyze you
with the power of my love.

Don't Run

When they hold you in the storm,
Keep you safe and warm,
And order your chaos with just one kiss—
Don't you be afraid…

Don't run.

Cake

Mouthwatering sweetness,
A delicious and decadent piece.
Just a sliver of the whole–
A slice of heavenly release.

Too rich for a healthy serving,
Too good for just one bite,
Too sweet to stay 'til morning,
But you'll stay for half the night.

You'll get just what you want,
But not what you deserve.
Come taste what you desire–
It tastes just like dessert.

Just indulge yourself a little–
Save some room before you're through.
Have yourself a little cake
And make sure you eat it too.

Lollipop

You're a candy-coated razor blade:
Each sweet lick is a dare.
And I wonder…
How many licks does it take
To get to the center?
I guess I'll know
When my tongue starts to bleed.

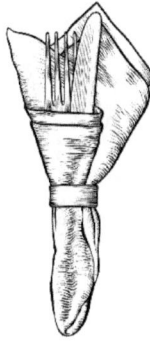

Napkins

Won't you come and take a seat?
And have yourself a very fine feast.

Don't you love how fresh and clean,
How neatly pressed and dressed I've been?

If you please, remove your cap,
And place me neatly in your lap.

Go ahead and make a mess–
I'll clean you up without protest.

Shake me off, toss me about.
Press me firmly– iron me out.

Lick your lips and tuck me in,
Just to use me once again.

Crumbs

He was rich,
I was poor,

I was starving,
Begging at his door.

He kept feeding me crumbs;
I kept coming back for more.

I Know What You Need

You need to lay your head on my breast
And hear the sound of my heart beating.
You need me to wrap my arms around you,
And hold you tight– treat you right.

You need to let the light of my love
Guide you out of the darkness.
You need to decompress, de-stress,
Let someone else take care of this mess.

You need to lay down the burdens
You've been carrying for so long,
Let them fall to the floor,
Close your eyes and shut the door.

You need to be reminded of why you're here–
The purpose of life– the reason is clear:
To feel the pleasure of unconditional love;
A treasure too often buried by fear.

Butterflies

You're in my dreams,
You're in my head,
You're in my mouth,
You're in my bed.

You're a freak between the sheets—
God damn, you're just my type!
You've slowly crept between the cracks
Of my well-fortressed life.

Tell me is this destiny,
Or another game to play?
Tell me if I should laugh or cry,
Stay or run away?

Tell me are you terrified
Of all I represent?
The Devil only preys on those
Of us who heaven sent.

Are you ready to let me in–
To let love conquer fear?
Are you ready to let go
Of the dreams you once held dear?

Can you release that white knuckled grasp
Clutching the known so tight?
For only open hands can catch
A butterfly landing from flight.

Atlas

You long to shrug,
But you can't—
You have too much to lose.

But,

A world of hurt,
And a world of pain
Is all you stand to gain.

Cinders

I long for you to love me,
To hold me,
To cherish me.
I long for a comfort that needs no words–
For a solace that comes
From the depths of the soul;
A feeling all pervasive,
All consuming,
Like fire,
To burn me up,
Bit by bit,
And leave me
Nothing but smoldering cinders.

I long to love you like that–
To hold you,
To cherish you,
To consume you.
To burn it all away,
Dance in the flames,
And reduce you
To a pile of ashes.
But you've already got someone,
Haven't you?
And anyway,
You're deathly afraid
Of getting burned.

Belonging

I don't belong in your world —
you belong in mine.
Let me pull you in,
show you everything I know about love;
about passion; about soul.

I don't belong in your world of make-believe;
pretty plastic people playing pitiful pretend.
You belong here with me–
in the realms of real-life fantasy
filled with fantastic freedom far beyond
your wildest dreams.

Don't you see that everything in your world
dies;
that everything in your world disappears?
Because it's not real.
You should know
what is real remains.

That's why you don't belong there anymore–
because with each breath you take with me,
with each step you take towards me,
you're becoming more real— can you feel it?
Your eyes are beginning to see what can't be
unseen:
        the truth.

Take my hand.
Let me lead you towards your home,
where your spirit is free to unfold in pleasure
and beauty;
a place where you've always belonged.
Darling, I don't belong in your world—

You belong in mine.

Perspective

You have
Money and power;

I have
Freedom and love.

Now tell me
Which of us is more wealthy?

Bloom

The more my flower
Opens and expands,
The more light I let in,
The more it falls
Through your hands.

Give It All Away

I just want to give it all away,
This love inside,
Passionate flames,
Burning, consuming, I'm trying to fight–

Longing for you to envelop me,
But your arms are full
Of another girl's dreams,
So no arms will hold me tonight.

You're a China shop,
I'm a raging bull.
You're a stone wall,
I'm a breeze that blows through.

Looking past her eyes to mine
What do you see
That you desire?
Why hold your hand in the fire?

Still, I stand by, biding my time,
Waiting for you to release us both
From this pain and pleasure,
Dance with dark and bright–

Each desires the other,
But, while you
Welcome the darkness,
I'm consumed with light.

Fantasy

My deepest, darkest fantasy
isn't the one where
you make my toes curl,
I grip the bedsheets
and scream your name...

My deepest, darkest fantasy
is the one where,
against all odds,

You stay.

Queen Of Hearts

What a fun little game
We're playing, you and I.
Dancing with the Queen of Hearts
And turning a blind eye

Just to glimpse behind the curtain,
A penny for your thoughts?
If we tried to run away
You know we'd just get caught.

A very curious cat and mouse,
Running round they go.
Nine lives to live with eight run down,
And only one to go.

Falling down a rabbit hole
A curiouser path to take,
A little fun never hurt no one,
Except for when they break.

We're both mad here, so
Show your cards and drink some tea.
If a raven is like a writing desk,
Then what does that make me?

Entirely bonkers, of that I'm sure,
Even a fool wouldn't be so trite!
A painted rose by another name
Would still smell just as nice.

When I play a game like this,
You know I have to grin.
No take backs, no do overs friend—
When I play, I play to win.

Toys

Used,
That's what I am.
Worn,
Certainly true.
Damaged,
But no worse for wear,
So I offer a price
You can't refuse.

I say:
See this pretty thing
Up on the shelf
Isn't it nice?
Don't you want to take me home?
Make me your own?
Play a game
And roll the dice?

Don't you
Want to
Possess,
Caress?
Confess
How you long
For something
So useless.

Just
A trinket,
A nick knack,
A silly little toy,
Yet it moves you,
Excites you,
Makes you feel
Like a little boy.

But just like that,
It will be over one day.
The fun will be gone,
You'll move on and play

With another fun distraction—
Something shiny and new,
And I'll go back on the shelf,
Just another toy to you.

Rag Doll

Pick your little rag doll
Up off of the shelf.
Stitch her little mouth shut
So she can't scream for help.

She's a little tattered,
And she looks like a mess…
She got a little dirty
When you took off her dress.

With her little round nose,
And her red fingertips,
She's so soft and pretty
With her little red lips.

Her hair is made of yarn,
She has buttons for eyes.
They always stare wide–
It seems she's always surprised.

She doesn't seem to mind
When you drag her around,
Toss her to the floor
And leave her waiting to be found.

Just hold her near your chest
When you're feeling scared and small.
She'll always be your comfort—
She's your little rag doll.

Ouroboros

See how I'm on my knees for you?
See how I beg and plead for you?
See how all I want and need is you?
That's the conundrum, isn't it?

See how I dress so nice?
See how I take it all off?
See how I let you inside?
That's truly naked, isn't it?

See how I long to transmute
Base metal into gold,
With a flame hot enough to combust
Burning in the crucible of my heart?

See how this game is a circle,
Never ending or winning–
Just a pair of foolish snakes
eating each other's tails?

See how alchemy is the only true way
To turn the tables and end the game?
See how infinity laid on its side
Turns from a circle to a sphere?

A Moon endlessly chasing her Sun;
A Goddess hopelessly fallen in love
With a mortal whose sword will slice
the heads of a thousand snakes,

only to watch them regrow.

Soulmates

We were as one,
though oft' we seemed
as though we'd gone astray.

The two of us near,
though far apart,
in separate bodies we dwelt and played.

He—a wolf,
howling at the moon,
and I—the moon at which he brayed.

Destiny

Next to you
is where I want to be.
By your side
is where I feel free.

Never mind
the changing tides,
the ruthless lies,
the where's and why's.

Never mind
the moans and sighs,
the hounds and flies,
the hellish cries.

Don't let them
keep you up at night.
Accept your plight,
and make it right.

I'll be waiting
near the fire,
The one that burns
white hot desire.

Patiently, like a good little girl,
waiting for your love to unfurl.
Waiting to see what's meant to be–
waiting for destiny to set us free.

Longing

I long only for your lips–
A simple wish
For your kiss…
Your tongue on mine–
It feels like bliss.

I dream only of you,
And when I do,
I wake up blue…
Each time I realize
That I'm not next to you.

L. O. V. E.

Last night I dreamt
Of our first kiss,
Violent and sweet;
Even now, makes me weak.

Sunrise

My favorite time
is sunrise–
new beginnings,
golden skies.

My favorite lies
are in your eyes–
my tummy flopping
with butterflies.

Right Where You Want Me

You've got me trained
not to ask questions;
not to talk about things that hurt;
not to ruin precious moments
with moot discourse,
and words that get us nowhere.

You've got me trained
to open my door and let you in;
to forget my anger
every time you kiss my lips;
to forget my pain
when you wrap your arms around me.

You've got me trained
to lose myself in you,
and to allow you to get lost in me;
just for a few brief moments,
just for a few short hours,
before it all fades back into nothing again.

Leaving

I've gotten so used
To watching you go,
To shutting the door
And being alone.

I've gotten so used
To saying goodbye,
To turning my back
So you can't see me cry.

I've gotten so used
To raising my head,
To an ache in my heart;
An empty space in my bed.

I've gotten so used
To a life without you,
To accepting the truth—
Leaving is all you'll ever do.

Why?

"You know it's wrong,
so why do you stay?" they asked.

"Fuck if I know," she answered.

"Probably because it feels better
than being alone."

Origami Cranes

Go ahead and write your lies
Neatly on the paper lines.

Pen your pretty promises
In gilded ink– crossed T's and dotted I's.

Tell me how much you love me,
And how much you need me too.

Tell me what I want to hear–
Make it compelling, like you always do.

Pour your fibs out from your ribs,
Scribble fancy fictions on the page,

Then fold them into paper planes,
Chinese stars, origami cranes,

And fly them, flick them, hang them up,
Watch the wind blow them all away–

Anything to erase the pain
Of knowing it was all in vain.

Fool's Gold

Fool me once,
Shame on you.
Fool me twice,
Deja vous.

Fool me now,
Like you fooled me then–
Don your mask
And play pretend.

A game of secrets,
Little white lies;
A flick of the wrist,
A clever disguise.

A shiny distraction,
A trick of the light–
Fleeting and fading,
But c'est la vie, right?

A riddle whose clue
Was plain from the start:
If you sawed it in two,
You'd slice half of a heart.

A magic trick,
A tall tale told,
A glimmer of hope;
A lump of fool's gold.

Hostage

I begged you to leave me alone,
and you wouldn't.
I told you to stay away,
but you couldn't resist.

I warned you that I wasn't like the others—
I told you my love was too deep,
and my heart was too fragile,
but you did it anyway.

You crept in like a thief in the night,
and stole my heart without paying the price.

Now you're holding me hostage again…
funny we both knew how this would end.

Nights

Nights are the hardest,
sitting on the couch alone.
Wishing you were here to hold me.
Wishing things could be different.
Wishing I didn't miss you,
knowing that nothing will ever change,
and all the wishing and longing
is just wasted energy.

So, I take another drink,
puff another smoke,
change the channel
and watch something else…
Desperately trying
to take my mind off of you.
Trying not to think
of what you're doing now.
Trying to forget
how safe I feel in your arms.

Why does it always feel so right
when we're together,
and so wrong
when we're apart?

Soon, I'll fall asleep and forget,
drifting into another world
where you can't follow me.
Sleep is the only reprieve I'll get.

Disappear Completely

"We gotta let it go," he said,
so I said Ok. I won't beg you stay–
you don't want my love?
I won't stand in your way.

Thanks for making me feel
like something was real;
for luring me in
just to shove me out again.

Thanks for leading me on,
sending me songs,
and breaking my heart
while saying you loved me.

You said that we're done,
that it's time to move on–
you've made it quite clear
that you don't need me.

So, for my final act,
I will show you how
I can disappear
completely.

Something Was Real

I'll never understand
why he let
our love die.

I swore that something was real,
but I guess it was all
just a lie.

Cold, Hard & Dead

I fell in love
with a married man.
He loved me too,
or so he said.

We shared our bodies,
minds, and souls,
and I was always happiest
when he was in my bed.

But of course, the day came
when he sent me away,
so, with tears streaming from my eyes,
I fled.

I wished him well,
as my sinking heart fell,
and plummeted to the Earth
    cold,
        hard,
           & dead.

Doctor

Calling a doctor,
Come ASAP!
I need medical assistance—
My heart's bleeding profusely.

Bring your little black bag,
Never mind a stethoscope.
It's not beating anyhow—
There's no fucking hope.

No need for lidocaine,
I'm already numb.
I can't feel anything—
The shock has just begun.

I'm pretty sure I'll be just fine
If you just stitch me up.
Put a clock where my heart once was
So I'll know when my time is up.

Silver Platter

"So many others will want to experience you,"
he said,

But the one I wanted most
was right there in my bed.

"I belong to you." I said,

But I got no reply —
he left me on read.

"Please don't do this…don't throw our love away!"
I begged,

But he showed how much he loved me
by leaving me instead.

Oz

You don't feel; you're dead inside.
You're not real; you're a robot with metal parts—
a Tin Man without a heart.
You're not alive, just animated
with the fake electricity of this world.
If I were to cut you, you wouldn't bleed—
you'd just stare at me blankly
and process a work order for Tuesday.

And me—I feel too much.
I'm a perpetual child filled with hope and wonder.
I'm a dark Dorothy,
with far too much magic for this world...
Always escaping to the other side,
dancing in the land of Oz,
sleeping in fields of poppies,
dreaming fantastic dreams,
and gallivanting with witches
and little people with lollipops.

Yet, we're both searching for something.
Both seeking, and never finding,
One bleeding, the other grinding.
I hope that we find the Wizard one day,
if we follow the yellow brick road.
Maybe you'll find a heart,
and I'll find my way
back home.

Fools

We are fools, you and I.
I'm a fool to love you,
And you're a fool to let me go.

Fairy Tales

You've got that Midas touch—
Every kiss turns me to gold.
Though it's never enough, I just want more,
But you're already sold.

What's a loveless life worth
With wealth and riches galore?
Do you enjoy that money stacked
With your back against the door?

That poison apple sparkles, shines;
Illuminates the dark corners of your mind.
You just can't wait to take a bite,
& kill your innocence just like Snow White.

Your million dollar castle up high on a hill,
Your princess wife that you just can't stand.
Your fairytale life that gives you a thrill—
You think *that* makes you a better man?

Don't you wish it made you love her?
Don't you wish it made her say
All the words you've longed to hear;
Relieve the pain you've kept at bay?

What's the price you'd pay for peace?
What's the magic number?
How much is enough for your woes to cease–
To wake Aurora from her slumber?

What's the cost of a weightless soul;
A life of love; a heart of gold?
What's the price you'd pay for that?
Go get your soul and buy it back.

Queen

How you gonna do me like that?
Push me away
Just to pull me right back?
Lift me up
Just to see me fall?
Back me in a corner,
Push me up against a wall?

Then act surprised
When I scream and fight,
Tell me I look cute
When I scratch and bite?
Tell me to put away my claws...
Please—
you haven't even seen them yet!
I think it's best you back away
Before you see just how deep they can get!

How you gonna treat me like
Another basic bitch?
How you gonna pretend like
I'm not the best you'll ever get?

You want to go?
There's the door.
Make like Tom Petty and
Don't come 'round here no more.
I'm tired of the lies,
Wiping tears from my eyes.
I'm not a happy meal toy–
A cheap plastic dollar prize.
Don't you know a Queen
When you see one?
Clearly you don't recognize.

Cheater

Little slips,
little lies;
I see right through
your disguise.

A simple question,
innocent laughter
tells me clearly
what you're after.

You don't need me–
you never did.
You just need a fantasy–
a hottie in your bed.

I'm just a means
to an end–
you think
that I don't know?

It's a low blow,
honey, but
you reap
what you sow.

I crave, but
can't have you;
you crave
and get me too.

All the while
I'm wondering…
How the hell
will I make it through?

Wine and weed
only do so much–
they take the edge off,
but I still miss your touch.

Now you're leaving me in tears.
It's not fair, to be clear,
but it's the game we chose to play,
and now it's over my dear.

Yo-Yo

He'd been stringing me along
since he sent that first song;
got me all up in my feels,
had me clicking my heels.

He spun me all around
just to drag me to the ground,
then he reeled me back in
just to wind me up again.

I wanted him to stay–
had me feeling some type of way,
instead, he dropped me at his feet
and watched me roll right down the street.

I was looped around his finger,
a lengthy piece of thread;
each time he walked the dog
he tricked me, made me scratch my head.

I loved it when he played with me,
and I wowed him with my tricks.
Like a nostalgic childhood memory,
I could never quite get my fix.

He tried to keep me in his pocket,
but I couldn't be contained;
everyone knows a tightly wound thread
is eventually bound to break.

Delete The Playlist

Didn't I give you all I had to give, babe?
This was no ordinary love,
and you threw it all away.

I can't keep crying, can't keep trying–
I've got to delete the playlist tonight.
You know I'm no good at goodbyes,

So, I'll see you in another life.

Haiku

Thanks for ruining
Two hundred favorite songs
Forever… *asshole.*

Gluttony

So, I see you're on to the next…
Shouldn't be surprised
You're moving on so soon.
Didn't wait long to replace me, did ya?
Didn't waste much time
Pouring salt in the wound.

You had your cake and ate it too;
Got just what you wanted—
Isn't that just like you?
But just one piece is never enough—
For someone who's insatiable,
Getting full's tough.
Gotta gorge on more & more,
Get a plate and fill 'er up!
Treat it like Thanksgiving—
Eat until you're stuffed.

Then double up and go again,
Unzip your pants
And make some room.
Lick your crumbs,
Clean your plate,
Devour all
You can consume.
Then sit back,
Kick up your feet,
And let the game
Resume.

Disposable

Did he think I was like plastic?
Just another side bitch?
Once he got his scratch itched,
He threw me in the garbage.

Did he think I was a happy meal?
Used me like a free refill:
Once he sucked me dry,
He left me for another cheap thrill.

Did he think I'd just get over it?
Beg him for another fix?
Close my eyes and pretend that
My lips were the only ones he'd kissed?

I thought my love could make him whole.
Turns out it was my heart he stole.
Left an empty space inside my soul…
Guess he thought I was disposable.

Mirrors

How many times do you fall asleep crying?
How many times do you feel like dying?
How many nights do you lie awake in bed,
Wild thoughts of *could have beens*
running through your head?

How many times do you
replay the words I said?
How many times do you wish
you'd stayed instead?
How many pretty lies did you have to tell
To wind up here, in your very own
self-created hell?

How many hearts have you broke in two,
my dear?
How many souls have you crushed
without a tear?
How many lovers have you left without a trace?
How many mirrors will you ever turn and face?

Easy

I said
  "I wish it was as easy for me as it is for you."

He said
  "I didn't say it was easy, I said it was best."

But darling, when it comes to love,
  Shouldn't "easy" and "best" be the same?

Best

He had to do
what was best for
him,
and that
didn't include
me.

The Truth

I had to face the truth:
I guess you just meant
more to me
than I did
to you.

Lost

I told you
I was lost without you,
and you told me
everything would be ok.

You lied.

It is not ok.

I am not ok.

Stained Glass

Your tongue
is so holy,
but it cuts me so deep–
each empty promise
that escapes your lips
makes me want to weep.

Your silence,
it chokes me
'til I can barely speak–
hold me under,
make me suffer;
turn the other cheek.

Your absence,
It stabs me,
a nail right through my heart–
each sinful day
you walk away,
it rips me apart.

Your confessions,
they kill me,
but I've made them into art–
a blood-stained glass cathedral;
A colored light
Within the dark.

Angels & Demons

It seems my love
wasn't enough
to save him from his demons.

He made an angel cry—
I guess
he must've had his reasons.

Stop Calling it Love

Stop calling it love
when you're just infatuated;
when you're just in lust,
when you're not all in or bust.

Stop calling it love
when you won't put in work;
when you don't want to stay,
and do whatever it takes.

Stop calling it love
when you dread going home;
when you're not satisfied,
so you creep on the side.

Stop calling it love
when your dick's in the dirt;
when you're out like a light,
and gone like the night.

Stop calling it love,
it's time to admit—
there's no love in your heart;
you're just playing the part.

Lies

Don't sit there and
tell me you love me
while simultaneously
breaking my heart.

Leave

"Just leave while you're ahead,"
she whispered.
"Leave my heart on the counter
and never look back."

When Love Dies

When love dies,
where does it go?

Does it hide in the couch cushions
with the loose change,
waiting among stale crumbs
to be found, brushed off,
and placed back in your pocket?

Does it swirl down the drain
with the bath water,
rinsed off with the soap suds,
never to be seen again?

Does it sit in the back of the closet
hanging there with all the old coats,
waiting for you to pull it out and
try it back on, hoping it still fits?

Does it evaporate
like steam;
dissipate into thin air,
leaving a smudge of moisture on the mirror,
fogging up the reflection
of who you used to be?

Can you give it CPR
and bring it back with a breath;
a few pumps on the chest,
a set of feverish lips
sweetly pressing
against the last straw of hope?

Or is it buried
six feet under,
covered in dirt,
watered with tears,
dissolved to bones,
never to be reborn again?

Enough

"You're so deep," he said,
but not deep enough
for him to dive beneath my waves.

"You're so beautiful," he said,
but not beautiful enough
to keep his gaze from wandering away.

"You're such a good girl," he said,
but not good enough
to make him stay.

Undertow

You pulled me under like a wave
When I was trapped in a great divide.
I thought *you* were the one I'd save,
But *I* was the one caught in your tide.

The more I tried to resist your lies,
The more I thrashed to escape the pain,
The more I sunk beneath your waves,
The more your current pulled me out again.

I let you drag me to your depths;
I showed you everything I know.
I held my breath, and held your hand,
But it was no match for your undertow.

Oh, My Love

I don't want to lose you–
I just want to use you
To indulge in my own dark needs.

But I don't want to keep you
From the people that need you,
So, I'll just sit here and bleed.

If I could, I'd trace
Every line of your palms
And tell your fortune
With a gypsy's grin.

If I could, I'd hold
Both your cheeks in my hands
And kiss you sweetly
Like an angel sent from heaven.

But what does it matter
When we're treading deep water
And the current keeps us at bay?

Oh, my love, it's wicked how
You've taken your love away.
Yet here I stand, a pitiful fool —
loving you anyway.

The Table

There the empty table sat,
Abandoned long ago.
It seemed to pine for a lover's fare
With candlesticks aglow.

I pressed the linen, crisp and clean,
And had the table set
With goblets, plates, and chinaware,
But I wasn't finished yet.

Candles, flowers, bread, and wine,
I gave it all I had–
Prepared a feast fit for a king,
Then called a hungry lad.

He said he'd be there right away–
As quick as he was able.
He'd love to dine with a lovely girl,
And gladly share her table.

He soon appeared, smiling wide,
Knocking on my door.
He pulled me close and kissed me deep–
Swooped my feet right off the floor.

He proclaimed that he was starving–
Couldn't stand it any longer.
So, he ate, and drank, and stuffed his face
To satiate his hunger.

Then he tossed his napkin on the ground,
Said he couldn't stay;
Grabbed his coat and tipped his hat,
And brusquely walked away.

I cleared the dishes, cleaned the mess,
Swept the crumbs up from the floor;
Wiped my tears as I sat and stared
At the empty table once more.

Fold

I put my cards on the table.
You folded and walked away.
So, why don't I feel
like I've won?

Haunted

You keep haunting my dreams;
they're a blessed reprieve
from the waking hell
of being alone.

Each time I awake,
I think it's a mistake,
'til I remember you're never
coming home.

Right As Rain

It's raining, it's pouring.
I keep waking up mourning.
Each morning I look for a ray of hope,
But it keeps storming.

I went to bed and bumped my head
And had a wicked dream:
You and I were right as rain,
And all was well, it seemed.

Then we kissed, and I felt your tongue
Claiming all of me.
I swooned, I moaned, I came undone–
I fell right to my knees.

But when the dream was over,
And I was fully woke,
I found myself in a cold, dark room
With my heart still fully broke.

So I laid back down and closed my eyes,
Tried to forget the pain.
Told myself that soon enough,
All would be as right as rain.

I Miss You

Tonight, it's raining,
and I miss you.
Tomorrow it may be sunny,
And I'll still miss you.

I'll miss you if it's cloudy.
I'll miss you if the sun is setting.
If the moon is dark or full,
it won't matter–
I'll miss you anyway.

But the real question is:
Will you miss me?

This Bed

This bed is still empty,
even when I'm in it.
It feels cold and wide;
mattress undented,
pillows unused,
sheets unwrinkled,
blankets sighing with lament
for a body not kept warm.

Though I lie awake,
I am not here–
I am in another world;
dreaming of your skin on mine,
remembering your scent; your strength.
Arms wrapped,
and legs intertwined;
sweat, and bliss, and heat;
sighs, and moans, and crescendos—
all things that should be still

In this bed.

Pirates

Freezing in the cold night air,
Wind whipping up my skirt,
A stormy eve to match my pain;
A twist of fate that hurt.

My hair in curls, strands of pearls,
Dress of lace in white,
My lover's gone, and so I'm on
A pirate's quest tonight.

He'd sailed the seas, spread my knees,
And gladly warmed my bed;
Flashed a grin and pinched my chin–
Said I'd soon be wed.

Then off he sailed into the sun
Setting in the West,
Ne'er to return, he left me here
Bleeding from my chest.

Now near this cliff I brace myself,
The raging sea below,
A seagull's cry the only sound
I hear before I go.

As I plunge into the murky depths,
Deliver me to my fate!
Davy Jones will wed his bride,
And I mustn't make him wait.

Poking

We're like children
who came across a dead squirrel on the
road.
"Is it really dead?" we wonder.
So, we grab our long sticks and begin to
poke.

It wiggles a bit.
The tail flops, and it moves ever so slightly.
It's not completely dead yet, but clearly,
it's on its way out.

We keep poking, prodding;
jabbing at our love with sticks.
"Is it really dead?" we wonder.

Each time we poke, it moves just a little,
becoming briefly animated
with the life it once contained.

But it's no use.
It's dying, you see,
and no amount of poking
will ever bring it back.

You Done?

I keep letting you in,
You keep coming around.
When I try to run away,
You keep chasing me down.

You like playing these games,
I like believing your lies.
You like messing with my head?
You like seeing me cry?

You done broke my heart
One too many times.
You done fucked me up
When you crossed that line.

You made it very clear
I'll never be your number one.
So, now I gotta ask:
You done?

And Still

Don't say you want me.
We both know that's a lie–
For can you want someone,
And still
Walk away
When you see them cry?

Don't say you need me.
We both know you're blowing smoke–
For how can you need someone,
And still
Give them up
When you were just that close?

Don't say you love me.
We both know that's not true–
For how can you love someone,
And still
Crush their heart
With the heel of your shoe?

Running In Place

Why did I let myself love you?
Why did I not run away
When I had the chance?
Now that chance is gone,
And here I am running in place.

Humpty Dumpty

I climbed the walls
You built so high,
Reached the top
And touched the sky.
It was blue, like your eyes
Open wide.

You told me you'd be there,
Told me you cared;
Then you pushed me down
With a cold hard stare.
You watched me fall,
Saw me lying broken,
Just like all your promises,
Took back the words spoken.

Now all of me is cracked
And battered,
Shards are strewn about
And scattered.
You have no horses,
You have no men;
You can never put me back
Together again.

This is goodbye forever–
I can't be your friend.
This is the final chapter.
Period.
The end.

Tell Me

Please tell me how
to stop loving someone?

Please tell me how you did it—
Please tell me how it's done?

Please tell me how to make my brain
forget the way I feel?

Please tell me how to make my heart
stop bleeding and start to heal?

Please tell me how to stop the pain
and feel joy once again?

I've heard that it's quite possible,
but if so, please tell me when?

It Wasn't You

I let a man text me,
And it wasn't you.

I let a man see me,
And it wasn't you.

I let a man touch me,
And it wasn't you.

I let a man kiss me,
And it wasn't you.

I let a man hold me,
And it wasn't you.

I told a man to leave me,
Because he wasn't you.

The Wolf & The Lamb

Of her scent on the breeze,
The wolf caught a good whiff,
So he followed a trail
That led down a steep cliff.

Through a sparkling river,
And a densely wooded glade,
He came to a meadow,
And stood enjoying the shade.

Then his eyes became narrowed,
His ears became perked;
His nose swiftly pointed
To where the little lamb lurked.

Tall grass she was eating
As she rambled about.
She had little pink ears,
And a little pink snout.

Hung 'round her neck
Was a little gold bell,
Its faint little tinkle
He could hear quite well.

She was all by herself,
There was no time to lose.
She must've strayed from her flock–
He knew he must make his move.

Then he circled around,
Slowly closing the gap.
Soon the little white lamb
Would fall right into his trap.

At last, he was ready
To pounce upon his prey,
But no sooner did he leap,
Did he wish he'd stayed away.

A mighty howl escaped his lips
As pain he deeply felt.
A bullet ripped right through his chest,
And pierced right through his pelt!

"We got him, girl!"
The farmer laughed, holstering his gun.
"It's stew again for supper,
And I like my wolf well done."

Tragic

Isn't it tragic,
This cruel twist of fate?
The love that once
Was in my heart
Has now turned into hate.

Love & Hate

I hate you,
I hate you,
I hate you!

I scream over and over in my head.

I love you,
I love you,
I love you.

My heart whispers back instead.

Jaded

"Is she jaded?" you ask.
Of course I am!
How could I not be?
I don't want to open up again–
The idea makes me sick.

Just the thought
Of letting someone in
Makes my skin crawl–
Makes me want to withdraw,
Become infinitesimally small.

So, I hide behind not one,
But two evil eyes
That glare "Come at me bro!"
I may look like an angel,
But I will make you cry–
Make you wish you'd never been born–
Make you want to shrivel up and die!

Is that what you wanted to hear?
Or did you want to hear me lie?
Smile sweetly and say I'm fine?
Pretend I've got loads of kindness
And energy to give to one more
Wart covered toad,
Hoping that if I kiss him
He'll turn into a prince…

No thanks.
I'm not going back
down *that* fucking road!

This is what I've become:
All claws and fangs,
Wrapped inside my rage
In a pretty cloak of solid jade.

Who is to Blame?

How could I say
That I hate him this way?

The truth is I hate
How I made him to blame
For my own dumb mistake,
Now I feel so ashamed.

I must confess the truth I hid:
I gave away the love I did.

My heart was a gift–
"He stole it!" I cried sadly.
But what I failed to mention
Was that I gave it gladly.

Hourglass

If it doesn't bother you
To let me slip through
Your fingers
Like sand in an hourglass;

If it doesn't kill you
To see me with someone new,
Let my memory
Fade from your grasp.

Fade To Black

Put your lips on mine;
Come and kiss me one last time.
Let the sweetness of our love
Soften the bitterness of goodbye.

Put your hands in mine;
Let me trace an invisible line
Across hands that couldn't hold my heart–
Let our fingers intertwine.

Put your arms around me;
Hold me tight and don't let go…
For at least a solid minute–
Count the seconds as they go.

Then turn around and walk away,
And don't you dare ever look back.
Watch it melt into the sunset;
Like the sky, let our love fade to black.

The Dock

There I stood,
searching, waiting,
longing for you to
come home to me.

There I sighed,
whispers fleeting,
speaking to the wind
of your memory.

There I cried,
weeping, wailing,
mourning the love
you took from me.

There I plunged,
naked, sinking,
drowning in the waters
of your legacy.

The Problem

The problem was
I loved him
Too much,
And he loved me
Not enough.

Special

"You're special," he said,
And I wanted to say
"Then don't walk away."

But instead,
All I said was
"Special-Ed."

I Won't Beg

I won't beg,
but why
won't you love me?

I won't cry,
just turn my eyes away
when you look at her.

I won't scream,
but I'll send you a song
that hints at my rage.

I won't ask,
just silently watch
and question your every move.

I won't call,
but I'll think of you often,
remembering the cadence of your voice.

I won't beg,
just pretend that
everything will be ok, eventually.

Unwoven

Unravel all the winding threads
that stitched us together.
Rip out all seams that were woven
through each of our hearts
every time we came near,
knowing we'd eventually fall apart.

Erase the messages, delete the texts,
delete the songs and pictures–
all the memories we shared,
wipe them off our phones,
and the white boards of our minds,
then fill those empty spaces
with pretty white lies.

Wipe the tears;
invisible trails
of what was never meant to be.

Fill the cracks in our hearts with cement;
Sealed like a tomb,
our dying love lain like a corpse.

What was once living flesh,
now only bones in a grave
to be buried and forgotten
for eternity.

Notes

Carefully placed
On the empty pages of my heart–
That's where I wrote your name
A thousand times over.

Each stroke
A delicate whisper on my lips.
Each word
A sweet melody sung by a choir.

Crumpled and tossed
Into the wastebasket
Of hopeless dreams–
That's where you ended up.

A million tearful wishes
On just as many northern stars,
Each one fizzled out
With the rising sun.

Don't Look

Why do you keep looking–
torturing yourself,
and me,
every time?

Don't look.
My curves make circles in your mind.
My smile hides my sadness...
I'm so good at showing my innocence–
It covers up the pain I hide.

Don't look
into my eyes–
they'll only pull you deeper
under my spell,
and you're trying to escape,
remember?

Don't look.
Quit picking at the scab.
Turn away and let it heal.
I'm nothing to you now–
I'm no longer naked,
I've put on my shell.
Just close your eyes,
and for heaven's sakes,

Don't look.

Love, Poetry, Longing

Love
is what I gave you,
in the sweetness
of my surrender,
and the tenderness
of my gentle touch.

Poetry
is what I wrote you;
little words
strung together,
like the pieces
of my broken heart.

Longing
is how I left you,
in the hopelessness
of my despair,
and the ending
of a doomed affair.

He Loves Me Not

He said, "I loved you,"
Not "I love you."
He loved me then,
Now he loves me not.

I asked "You did…
But then what happened?"
He simply answered
"I cannot."

Get Away

You've got to get
away from here.
Run fast, run far,
far away my dear.

He doesn't love you—
he never did.
I know the truth hurts,
but that's life, kid.

Don't think it was your fault.
Please don't blame yourself.
You gave it all you could and now,
there's really nothing else

To give, to say, to do,
but move right on and get right out
Of this self-created hell
you're only making hotter for yourself.

Don't keep
burning, longing, waiting.
Don't keep
hoping, wishing, praying.

It's all for naught—
don't you see my dear?
That's why you must
get away from here.

Let You Lose Me

How can I just
let you lose me?
How can I just
give up?

How can I leave
a love so deep
I can never
get enough?

Oel Ngati Kamei

You said *"I see you."*
And we both knew what that meant.
It was beautiful,
And scary
To be seen like that…
But I liked it,
And I let you see me anyway.

I saw you too–
You had a certain gleam in your eye
That reminded me of fire;
You could make me burn
With just a look.
Burning with you
Was a beautiful pain.

And your smile–
It reminded me of heaven,
And all I wanted was to be let inside
The pearly gates of your heart.
I would have died a thousand times
Just to spend
Another day there with you.

I saw you,
And everything
You tried to hide.
It couldn't be hidden
When you looked in my eyes,

Even though you tried the most
To hide it from yourself.

I saw you
Struggling to keep your head above water,
Flailing in a sea of dying hopes,
And impossible dreams,
Wrapping the noose around your own neck,
And stepping up on the box
Of all their expectations.

I saw you
Backing away,
And running from your problems,
Into my arms,
Until you ran from me too—
Because just another problem
Is what I'd become to you.

Then you couldn't see me anymore,
Like you did before,
Because your vision was clouded
By all you tried to hide.
But I still saw you,
And that made it harder—
So much harder
To say goodbye.

A Pen Gone Dry

I've wanted to send you
a hundred songs;
all of them could say
more than I ever could.

I've wanted to die
a hundred times;
felt the stabbing of each word
like a nail in wood.

I've wanted to hold you
a hundred times more,
and wanted to hate you
more than ever before.

I've bitten my tongue
so hard I tasted blood.
I faced the pain in the pouring rain;
let my tears mix in with the mud.

But, my love will not die,
as much as I try,
so, I sit by and write this goodbye—
a tear-stained letter
with a pen gone dry.

Goodbye My Love

Leave me now.
Walk away and never look back.
Take all of our memories
In a hobo's knapsack.

Get to kicking rocks
Down that old dirt road–
The one that leads away from me
Into the great unknown.

In truth, I would have walked beside you,
And stayed right by your side.
Instead, you chose a different path—
You chose a life of lies.

So with you now, I cannot go,
And here you cannot stay.
So I'll say goodbye my love,
And send you on your way.

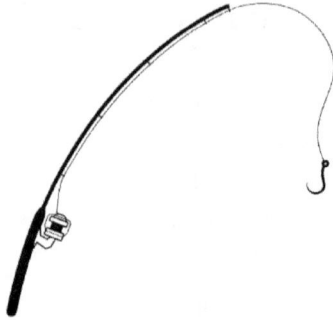

Fishin'

One dark,
moonlit night,
I took my pole out fishin'
by the lakeshore side.

I wished on a star,
and cast my line wide,
hopin' I'd find
a big fish that'd bite.

But wouldn't ya know,
I wound up cryin',
'cuz I hooked a big bullfrog that was lyin'
'neath the cold dark waters dyin'.

There was nothin' I could do
to save him—
he was halfway dead,
and too weak to leap or swim,

So I threw him back
in the cold dark lake;
left him to die alone
and suffer his fate.

My line was love–
I'd wished for a sign.
I thought this could be it,
but the timin' wasn't right.

Now I'm reelin' in my love,
windin' up the line...
'Fraid I didn't catch nothin'
this time.

Grief

They say that grief is love
with nowhere to go,
but I think grief is love
that can't be returned.

Let Them Go

When I said, "I love you," I didn't mean "sort of."
I didn't mean part-time, only on weekends.
I didn't mean the type of love you have
for your distant cousins, a childhood friend,
or the kind you feel for your mother-in-law.

When I said, "I love you," I meant the type of love
that makes you walk through fire;
The kind that keeps you up at night with a sick
child;
The kind of love that radiates from the cells like
photons; like a light switch that can't be shut off.

When I said "I love you," I meant that my soul
loves you, because that is the "I" that loves.
Not this ego, not this body,
but the ephemeral spirit that comes into existence
and dissolves back into nothing again.

When I said "I love you," I meant it—
And that's why I'm walking away.
Because sometimes love is leaving.
Sometimes love is knowing when to say goodbye.
Sometimes love is allowing someone
to be where they're at,
and loving them even if you can't stay there.
Sometimes the most loving thing you can do for
someone else is
to let them go.

Nothing

There's nothing much
That you can do
When you love them
More than they
Love you.

Anyway

He didn't love me enough
To stop him from leaving me here.

He didn't love me enough
To stay and wipe my tears.

He didn't love me enough
To keep him from walking away.

He didn't love me enough,
But I loved him too much anyway.

Turn The Page

Come and glimpse inside her cage,
Black with beauty, crimson with rage.
You praise and celebrate her strength,
While she smiles and bleeds, numb with pain.

Is it a blessing, or a curse–
To have a mind that puts him first,
To have a heart that loves him still,
To have a hole
That can never be filled?

How can she stand so tall?
How can she never fall?
How can one
Who's been so broken
Seem to rise above it all?

To raise her head and seize the day,
To love herself and heal the pain,
To fill that hole from deep within–
To turn the page and start again.

See Me

He's never going to see me,
see my stories, or my poems.

He's never going to see me breaking;
see my words ripped from my heart
and scattered among empty pages.

He'll never see my naked form
lying open and exposed on the bed,
or hear my voice sweetly calling his name.

He's never going to feel me
holding his hand or caressing his cheek.

He'll never see my eyes peering intently
into his.

He will never catch a moment glittering
with feeling,
unveiling my love and my soul
ever again.

Have I Moved On?

Of course, I've moved on.
I've planted seeds in the dirt
And watched them grow.

I've written words on pages
And gone about my business.

I've tended to the kids, the dog, the house,
Taken hot baths,
And seen numerous sunsets.

I've moved through the days, the nights,
The weeks, the months…
Onward, ever onward—

But how can I help it
If a piece of me was left behind?

Have You Forgotten Me Yet?

Day by day,
Is it getting easier
To let the memories fade?

That little voice,
Is it getting quieter–
The one that calls my name?

The life you live–
Is it getting happier
Without me in the way?

Do Good Men Exist?

Mother told me
"Find a good man,"
one who'd treat me right.

If I made sure
to be a good girl
he'd make my life *real* nice.

She said,
"Don't pick one like your Father–
Don't let him beat you down.

If he drinks and smokes
and runs his mouth
be sure to turn around."

She said,
"Keep your knees together.
Try not to make a fuss.

Grit your teeth,
and be polite,
and smile when you want to cuss."

So, I found some good men
who liked my smile;
they liked my body too—

But they liked the other girls more,
and so,
there was nothing I could do.

Then I found some good men
who solemnly swore
they liked me for my mind.

They swore they'd never
make me cry–
swore they'd love and treat me right.

But I found myself
with tear-stained cheeks;
crumpled wads of tissues in my hand,

Bruises on
my skin and heart,
wind singing in my ears as I ran.

I wondered "What is love?"
It feels like pain– an empty heart
that always has a crack.

I had gotten so good
at giving love away
to men who didn't want to give it back.

I was such a good girl;
I did as I was told,
but it didn't get me treated like I should.

It never did stop me
from getting used and hurt
by bad men who pretended to be good.

I Lied

I said I deleted the playlist,
but that was a lie.

How could I delete
nearly two hundred songs,
and over ten hours of music
that was our love language?

Those songs are all I have left,
besides a few rare pictures,
and a handful of fading memories.

Tonight

Tonight, I'm drinking water instead of whiskey.
I'm wiping beads of sweat from my brow
instead of tears from my eyes.

Tonight, I'm noticing how my skin
is just as soft as my heart,
how my love is still lingering like perfume
in the air around me;
a barely detectable scent
that is distinguished only by its hints
of delicate sweetness and floral notes.

Tonight is not like other nights,
crying myself to sleep
with alcohol still on my breath,
or desperately finding a myriad of distractions
to shift my mind away
from the heartache and loneliness.

Tonight, I'm sitting in silence,
listening to the distant tinkle of wind chimes
contrast against the faint ticking
of the clock on my wall.

I'm realizing that being alone with myself
is not the same as being alone;
that I've been dreading this moment,
 because I didn't want to admit the truth.

The truth is, I am always alone,
but I am rarely alone with myself,
because I am always paying attention
to something else.

I am rarely in the present moment,
because I am too often thinking
about the past or the future.

This present moment isn't so bad.
I'm alive. I'm breathing.
My heart is still beating.
My senses are all working.
I have so much to be grateful for,
and I finally realize that
this precious present moment
is all there is.

It dawns on me that tonight is a gift,
and so am I.

The Goddess

I am the storm,
raging and wild.

I am the night,
a howling moon child.

I am the Goddess,
powerful and sweet.

I am the Earth
rumbling beneath your feet.

I am the volcano
full of fire and rage—

Watch me turn on a dime,
take back all the love I gave.

Everything

In this moment
I finally accept
that I am
nothing
to him,
But I am
everything
to me.

Purpose

My purpose is not to be loved.
It's to
BE
Love.

Picking

I've always been a picker.
When I was small, I picked at my scabs until
they bled; I don't know why.
Maybe it's because I could control the pain.

The scab never felt like a part of me.
I wanted to see what was underneath.
The real parts were the parts that bled—
the parts that hurt.

I've always been bad at picking…
Picking the right partners,
the right choices, the right words to say.
I've always been so focused on doing the
picking that I never let myself be picked.

So now, instead of picking, I'm healing.
Instead of picking, I'm surrendering.
Instead of picking my scabs I'm noticing–
Noticing how it feels to be uncomfortable.
Noticing how it feels to hurt and heal slowly;
to be where I'm at; to not be in control.

I'm accepting that my life is constantly
unfolding
into pain and beauty and back again.
Over and over, the cycle continues,
and I will not pick
anymore.

What I Want

I want distant mountain ranges,
Crops and farmers' pastures,
Red and white barns full of hay bales,
& green and yellow John Deere tractors.

I want a wrap-around porch on an old farmhouse
To sip cool lemonade on a hot summer's day,
With big shade trees and thick green grass–
a place to watch the grandkids play.

I want to watch snow pile up on an old wooden
fence post;
Marvel at fields covered in a blanket of white.
Smell a fresh cut pine tree in my living room;
See faces all smiling at the sight.

I want to watch the sunset colors fade,
And paint the sky with light;
Catch fireflies in a mason jar,
Dance to crickets singing songs in the night.

I want to warm my hands over a crackling fire,
Watch shooting stars streak across the sky;
Double over with a belly full of laughter,
Catch a smile from a stranger passing by.

I want to lay my head on a beating heart–
One that beats for me.
I want to close my eyes, and fall asleep,
And wake up with my love beside me.

On To the Next

I bled, I cried, I almost died
From a broken heart that wouldn't quit.
But now, thank God, I'm moving on–
I can honestly say I'm over it.

It's true I wasted so much time
Losing myself in you.
I'm so relieved I finally grieved,
And somehow, I'm getting through.

Ok, I'm done, you're not the one–
I get it now, though it took me a while.
I'm sure you know– you let me go
With a hug, a kiss, and a smile.

So now, I guess I'll do the same,
Though it's just in a simple text.
Let this be my final goodbye—
Wish me luck as I move on to the next.

Happy

You'll be happy to know
That I'm letting him go.
You'll be happy to hear
I'm not keeping him near.

I'm happy to say
That I'm finding my way.
I'm happy to see
Love is setting me free.

Be happy for me
That I'm letting it be.
I didn't know then
I'd be happy again.

One Day

Maybe one day
I'll find someone who
Won't want to ever let me go.

Maybe one day
I'll find someone who
Won't ever leave me alone.

Tattoo

I'm getting another tattoo–
One that reminds me of you.
I'm hoping the pain that I'll feel
Will remind me
That wounds do heal.

I'm hoping this permanent ink
Will remind me to stop and think
Before I let myself fall
for someone who
Can't love me
The way I loved you.

Broken Open

He didn't break me—
He broke me open.
He helped me see that what was within me
Was so much more beautiful
Than what was outside.

He broke my heart,
But he didn't break my soul,
Even though it felt that way at times,
At my lowest;
I didn't know if I could find the strength
To carry on.

He broke my trust,
But renewed my trust in myself,
By reminding me of my worth,
My value,
And my unbreakable desire
For truth, honesty, integrity, and love.

He broke his promises,
But he helped me make a promise to myself:
To never settle for less love,
Less truth,
Less time or attention.

I see now
What I couldn't see then—
All this love I have to give
Was stuck inside me,
Trapped by my fears,
And old stories of who I thought I was,
And who I was supposed to be.

Even though I felt so broken,
He didn't break me—
He just broke me open.
And broken open
Is a beautiful place to be.

You Will Be Ok

In the dark night of the soul,
the light called to me like a beacon.
"You will be ok," it whispered.

I knew then
that I'd somehow survive;
that I'd somehow make it through.

The End

Leaving you with
Only a few
Very small
Everythings.

ABOUT THE AUTHOR

Crystle Castle is a writer, editor, and poet from
Boise, Idaho.
She enjoys putting a contemporary spin on the
classic romantic themes of love and heartbreak.

Inspired by the nursery rhymes and fables of her
childhood, she strives to stimulate the minds and
imaginations of her readers by combining allegory
and fantasy with an adult twist.

Her works often have a double entendre, a
hidden message, and a nugget of wisdom for the
reader. Those who care to read between the lines
will inevitably find deeper meaning in her words.

Follow her on Instagram: @electricgirlpoetry
Web: www.electricgirlpoetry.com

INDEX